flavored
breads

flavored
breads

LINDA COLLISTER
photography by
PATRICE DE VILLIERS

RYLAND
PETERS
& SMALL
LONDON NEW YORK

Art Director **Jacqui Small**

Art Editor **Penny Stock**

Editor **Elsa Petersen-Schepelern**

Photography **Patrice de Villiers**

Food Stylist **Linda Collister**

Stylist **Hannah Attwell**

Production **Kate Mackillop**

To Stevie

Notes: Ovens should be preheated to the specified
temperatures—if using a fan-assisted oven, adjust time and
temperature according to the manufacturer's instructions.

Most of the breads in this book can be frozen for up to
1 month. The exceptions are Bacon and Walnut Fougasses
(page 12), Cherry Tomato Focaccia with Basil (page 16),
Rye and Caraway Loaf (page 29), and Multi-seed Bread
(page 35), which should not be frozen.

First published in the USA as *Basic Baking Flavored
Breads* in 1997
This paperback edition published in 2003 by
Ryland Peters & Small, Inc.
519 Broadway, 5th Floor, New York, NY 10012

10 9 8 7 6 5 4 3 2 1

Text © Linda Collister 1997, 2003
Design and photographs © Ryland Peters & Small
1997, 2003

Library of Congress Cataloging-in-Publication Data

Collister, Linda.
  Flavored breads / Linda Collister ; photography by
Patrice de Villiers.
      p. cm.
  ISBN 1-84172-532-3
  1. Bread. I. Title.
  TX769 .C564 2003
  641.8'15–dc21

                                  2002154623

Printed and bound in China.

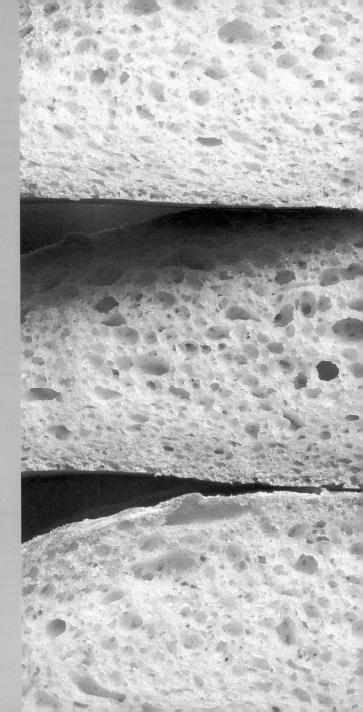

flavored breads **6**

mediterranean flavor **10**

spices and seeds **22**

special grains **36**

fruit and nuts **44**

vegetables and cheese **54**

index **64**

CONTENTS

flavored
breads

With such exotic, ever-changing variety on the supermarket shelves, why make bread? It saves money, of course, and has a taste and texture worlds away from even the best you can buy. You need no special talent—just flour, yeast, salt, water, a baking tray, an oven, and time. Much of the flavor in homemade bread comes from quality flours. Top row from left is **spelt**, higher in protein with more vitamins and minerals than ordinary flours. **Whole-wheat flour** with added bran makes a light, textured loaf with nutty flecks. **White bread flour** can be mixed with other flours, such as rye, to lighten them. Bottom row, from left, is **stone-ground whole-wheat flour**, which makes a chewy, coarse-textured loaf. **Stone-ground rye flour** used to be a staple in Eastern and Central Europe, but is now usually mixed with wheat flour, or added to sourdoughs for extra flavor. **Rising agents** used in breads include active dry yeast (top right) and compressed yeast (below right). When wrapped in plastic, compressed yeast can be refrigerated for a week or frozen for a month. When you make bread, dried yeast is mixed with flour: compressed yeast with liquid, usually water.

The flavor of dough comes from basic flours (for example, below from left, plain white or whole wheat flour), or from additions such as poppy seeds, rye flour or walnuts.

The quantity of **liquid** needed to form the dough depends on the condition of the flours, the type of flavorings, and even the weather. The ideal texture is soft but not sticky—add extra flour or water to achieve that consistency.

Salt is also crucial. If too little, the dough will rise too fast, then collapse: too much will inhibit or even kill the yeast.

Thorough **kneading** is vital. It develops gluten, the substance in the flour that acts as scaffolding supporting the bubbles of carbon dioxide from the yeast. It also ensures that the yeast is evenly distributed through the dough so it rises uniformly. You can knead by hand, or in a mixer fitted with a dough hook, but not in a food processor.

When dough is left to rise uncovered, it forms a dry crust and this can result in hard lumps in the baked loaf. So always cover your rising dough with a damp cloth or a large plastic bag.

Too little **rising time** produces a heavy, small

loaf. Too much is even worse: dough seriously distended by too long or too quick a rise will collapse in the oven.

Preheating the oven is important and requires care. A hot oven kills yeast quickly and prevents over-rising. Every oven has its own personality, so check shelf positions in your handbook and take my cooking times as guidelines, particularly with convection ovens. To test whether a loaf is cooked, unmold it and knock on the bottom with your knuckles: it should sound hollow. If it doesn't, replace and bake it for five more minutes before testing again.

Baked bread should be removed from the tray or pan and **cooled** on a wire rack; this helps form a good crust. For the best results, **slice** bread only when it's completely cool. Invest in **high quality** loaf pans and baking trays. They won't warp or scorch in a hot oven, they clean up well without rusting, and last a lifetime as well.

MEDITERRANEAN FLAVOR

bacon and walnut
fougasses

1 tablespoon olive or vegetable oil

3 oz. rindless bacon, finely diced

⅔ cup walnut pieces,
coarsely chopped

4⅔ cups unbleached
white bread flour

2 teaspoons sea salt

¾ cake compressed yeast,
crumbled*

1¼ cups lukewarm water

1 egg, beaten

3 tablespoons olive oil

extra flour, for dusting

extra oil, for brushing

several baking trays, greased

Makes 8 pieces

*To use active dry yeast, add
1 package to the flour when you
add the salt.*

Heat the oil in a skillet, add the bacon, and sauté until golden and crisp, but not hard. Drain on paper towels, then combine well with the walnuts.

Put the flour and salt in a large bowl, mix well, then make a well in the center. In a small bowl, cream the yeast to a smooth liquid with the water. Tip into the well, then mix in the egg and olive oil.

Gradually work in the flour to make a soft but not sticky dough. If there are crumbs in the bottom of the bowl, add water, 1 tablespoon at a time, until the dough comes together. If the dough sticks to your fingers, work in more flour, about 1 tablespoon at a time.

Turn out the dough onto a lightly floured work surface and knead thoroughly for 10 minutes until the dough feels smooth, very elastic, and silky.

Place in a lightly oiled bowl and turn it over so the entire surface is lightly coated with oil.

Cover with a damp cloth and let rise at room temperature until doubled in size—about 1½ hours. Punch down the dough, then turn out onto a lightly floured surface. Knead in the bacon and nuts until evenly distributed.

Weigh the dough and divide into 8 equal parts. Using a rolling pin, roll each piece into an oval about 8½ x 5 x ½ inch. With a sharp knife, cut about 8 slits in a herringbone pattern in each oval. Arrange them, spaced well apart, on the baking trays.

Lightly cover the baking trays with a damp cloth and let rise at cool to normal room temperature until doubled in size—about 45 minutes.

Uncover, lightly brush with oil, then bake in a preheated oven at 400°F for about 15 to 20 minutes until golden brown. Cool on a wire rack.

Variation

Salami Fougasses

Omit the bacon and walnuts. Skin a 3½ oz. piece of *saucisson sec* or salami, dice finely, and add after the first rising. Proceed as in the main recipe.

These **attractive**, *oval, individual loaves come from Provence where, these days, they are made* **plain** *or* **flavored** *with olives, herbs, charcuterie, or even candied fruit. Use top-quality bacon—poitrine fumée or dry-cured, thick-cut, and smoked.*

*This dough is risen **three** times. For an open, light **texture**, don't overload with olive oil.*

focaccia
with rosemary and sea salt

¾ cake compressed yeast, crumbled*

1⅛ cups water (room temperature)

6–7 tablespoons virgin olive oil

2 teaspoons sea salt

2 tablespoons finely chopped fresh rosemary, plus extra sprigs

about 3⅓ cups unbleached white bread flour

2 teaspoons coarse sea salt

extra flour, for dusting

extra oil, for greasing bowl

a 14 x 10-inch roasting or baking pan, greased

Makes 1 loaf

*To use active dry yeast, add 1 package with the chopped herb. Put all the liquid into the bowl at once and proceed with the recipe.

In a small bowl, cream the yeast to a smooth liquid with half the water. Add 3 tablespoons oil and the remaining water. Add the salt, chopped rosemary, and half the flour. Beat into the liquid with your hand. When combined, work in enough of the remaining flour to make a soft but not sticky dough.

On a lightly floured surface, knead for 10 minutes until very smooth and silky (or for up to 5 minutes at low speed in a mixer fitted with a dough hook). Put into a lightly oiled mixing bowl, turning it over so the entire surface is coated with oil. Cover with a damp cloth and let rise at cool to normal room temperature until doubled in size—about 2 hours.

Punch down the dough, turn out, then shape into a rectangle. Press into the bottom of the pan, pushing into the corners, and patting out to make an even layer. Cover and let rise as before until almost doubled in height—45 minutes to 1 hour. Flour your fingertips and press into the risen dough to make dimples ½ inch deep. Cover and let rise until doubled in height —about 1 hour. Press rosemary sprigs into the dimples and fill with olive oil. Sprinkle with sea salt.

Bake in a preheated oven at 425°F for 20 to 25 minutes until golden brown. Cool on a wire rack.

focaccia with pancetta

additional ingredients:

3½–5½ oz. pancetta or bacon

about 3 tablespoons
extra-virgin olive oil

sea salt and coarsely
ground black pepper

a 14 x 10-inch roasting
or baking pan, greased

Makes 1 loaf

Follow the recipe on the previous page, omitting the rosemary and sea salt.

During the first rising, broil the pancetta or bacon, and discard any rind and small pieces of bone. Drain and cool on paper towels, then chop finely and sprinkle with coarsely ground black pepper.

Punch down the risen dough and knead in the pancetta or bacon. Roll out the dough to fit the pan, then proceed as in the main recipe, drizzling with olive oil to fill the dimples and sprinkling with sea salt and coarsely ground black pepper. Bake, then cool, as in the main recipe.

cherry tomato focaccia with basil

additional ingredients:

5 oz. ripe fresh cherry tomatoes

a large bunch of fresh basil

4 tablespoons extra-virgin olive oil

sea salt and black pepper

a 14 x 10-inch roasting
or baking pan, greased

Makes 1 loaf

Follow the recipe on the previous page, omitting the fresh rosemary and sea salt.

Cut the tomatoes in half and strip the leaves from a large bunch of fresh basil. Just after making the dimples, push a basil leaf into each hollow, then half a tomato, cut side up. Cover the dough and let rise as before until doubled in height—about 1 hour.

Drizzle with olive oil to moisten the tomatoes and sprinkle with salt and pepper. Bake, then cool, as in the main recipe.

*Two **variations** on the main focaccia recipe.*

For a **sharper** *flavor, use pitted green olives.*

italian ciabatta
with olives and thyme

Put the olives in a bowl with the olive oil, lemon peel, and thyme. Cover and let marinate for 3 to 4 hours or overnight. Put 3½ cups flour in a large bowl and make a well in the center.

In a small bowl, cream the yeast to a smooth liquid with ½ cup water, pour into the well, then add the remaining water. Mix to a sticky dough, almost like batter.

Cover with a damp cloth and let rise at normal room temperature for 3 to 4 hours. It should grow to about 3 times its original size. Check occasionally to make sure the dough has not stuck to the cloth. Punch down the risen dough. Strain the olives, discard the lemon peel, and reserve the oil. Mix the oil and salt into the dough, then gradually work in the remaining flour to make a soft, sticky dough.

Cut in half and put 1 portion into another bowl. Mix half the olives into each. Cover with damp cloths and let rise as before until doubled in size—about 1 hour.

Tip onto a baking tray. Shape into 2 rectangles, 1 inch thick. Push the olives back into the dough, sprinkle with flour, and let rise uncovered at room temperature until doubled in size— about 1 hour. Bake in a preheated oven at 425°F for about 30 minutes until the loaves are brown and sound hollow when tapped underneath. Cool on a wire rack.

1 cup black olives, preferably kalamata, pitted

⅔ cup virgin olive oil

a strip of fresh lemon zest

3 teaspoons chopped fresh thyme

4⅔ cups unbleached white bread flour

1¾ cakes compressed yeast, crumbled*

1¾ cups water from the cold tap

2½ teaspoons sea salt

extra flour, for sprinkling

2 baking trays, well greased

Makes 2 loaves

*This recipe is not successful made with active dry yeast.

For this **Italian-style** *loaf, use well-flavored olive oil and good-quality, stone-ground, organic flour.*

olive oil bread

6⅔ cups unbleached white bread flour

3½ teaspoons sea salt

1 cake compressed yeast, crumbled*

about 2¾ cups water, at room temperature

½ cup extra-virgin olive oil

extra flour, for dusting

a large baking tray, lightly greased

Makes 1 large loaf

*To use active dry yeast, add 1½ packages to the flour with the salt, then proceed with the recipe.

Combine the flour and salt in a large mixing bowl and make a well in the center.

In a small bowl, cream the yeast to a smooth liquid with 3 tablespoons of the water. Pour into the well in the flour, adding most of the remaining water. Quickly mix the flour into the liquid, then pour in the oil and continue mixing until the dough comes together. Gradually add the rest of the water if necessary—the dough should be fairly soft, but should hold its shape and not stick to your fingers.

Turn out onto a lightly floured surface. Knead thoroughly for 10 minutes until the dough is elastic and smooth. Place in a large bowl, cover with a damp cloth, and let rise at cool to normal room temperature until doubled in size—about 2 hours. Turn out onto a floured surface. Do not punch down or knead, but gently shape the dough into a 22-inch-long sausage. Join the ends to make a ring. Transfer to the prepared baking tray, cover with a damp cloth, and let rise as before until almost doubled in size—about 1 hour.

Uncover the loaf, dust with flour, and bake in a preheated oven at 450°F for 10 minutes. Reduce to 375°F and bake for another 20 minutes or until it sounds hollow when tapped underneath. Cool on a wire rack.

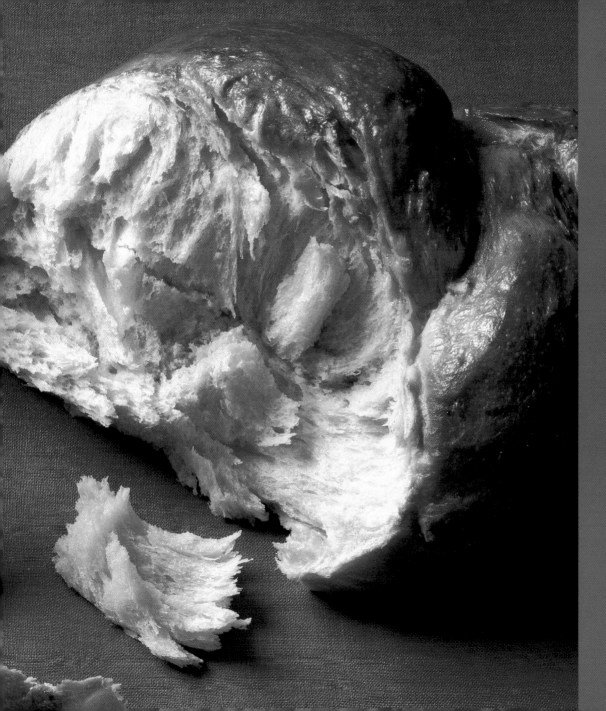

saffron braided loaf

1 heaped teaspoon
saffron threads

⅔ cup warm water

4⅔ cups strong
white bread flour

3 teaspoons sea salt

1 teaspoon sugar

2 tablespoons sweet butter,
chilled and diced

¾ cake compressed yeast,
crumbled*

1¼ cups skim milk,
at room temperature

1 egg, beaten

extra flour, for dusting

1 egg beaten with a
good pinch of salt, to glaze

a large baking tray, greased

Makes 1 large loaf

, *To use active dry yeast, add
1 package to the flour with the
salt and sugar, then proceed with
the recipe.

Toast the saffron on a plate in the oven at 350°F, without
burning, for 10 to 15 minutes, then crumble into a bowl. Add
the warm water, stir, cover, and let soak overnight.

Next day, combine the flour, salt, and sugar in a large mixing
bowl. Add the butter and rub in with your fingertips until the
mixture looks like breadcrumbs. Make a well in the center of
the mixture, then pour in the bowl of saffron.

In a small bowl, cream the yeast with the milk until smooth.
Stir in the egg, then pour into the well. Work the mixture to
form a fairly firm, soft dough. If any dry crumbs remain, work
in extra milk, 1 tablespoon at a time. If the dough sticks to
your fingers, work in extra flour, 1 tablespoon at a time.

Turn out onto a floured surface and knead thoroughly for
10 minutes (or 5 minutes at low speed in a mixer fitted with a
doughhook). The dough should be very elastic and silky
smooth. Put into a lightly greased bowl and turn it over so the
surface is lightly coated with oil. Cover with a damp cloth and
let rise at normal room temperature until doubled in size—
about 1½ hours.

Punch down the dough with your knuckles, then turn out on a
floured surface. It should be pliable but not soft, and should
hold its shape well. If not, knead in a little more flour.

Weigh the dough, divide into 3 or 4 equal pieces, and braid as
described opposite. Cover with a damp cloth and let rise at a
cool temperature until almost doubled in size—about 1 to
1½ hours. Don't let it over-rise or become too soft in a warm
place or it will spread.

Brush the top with egg glaze, then bake in a preheated oven at 450°F for 15 minutes until golden. Reduce to 440°F and bake for 20 to 30 minutes until it sounds hollow when tapped underneath. Cool on a wire rack.

To make a 3-strand braid:

Using your hands, roll 3 pieces of dough into ropes 16 inches long. Place the 3 ropes on the baking tray, then braid loosely together. Avoid overstretching the dough. Tuck the ends under to give a good shape.

To make a 4-strand braid:

Using your hands, roll 4 pieces of dough into ropes 13 inches long and 1 inch thick. Pinch them firmly together at one end, then arrange vertically in front of you, side by side, slightly apart, with the join at the top. Run the far-left strand under the 2 middle ones, then back over the last it went under. Run the far-right strand under the twisted 2 in the middle, then back over the last it went under. Repeat until all the dough is braided. Pinch the ends together at the bottom. Transfer to a baking tray, tucking the ends under to give a neat shape.

*Saffron gives a rich gold color and a deep, **aromatic** flavor to bread dough. The longer the saffron is soaked, the better.*

Made to celebrate the Jewish sabbath, this rich, sweet bread can be flavored with honey, saffron, or spices.

vanilla challah

1 cup skim milk

2 tablespoons sugar

1 vanilla bean, split lengthwise

¾ cake compressed yeast, crumbled*

4⅔ cups unbleached white bread flour

2½ teaspoons sea salt

¾ stick sweet butter, melted and cooled

3 eggs, beaten

extra flour, for dusting

vegetable oil, for greasing

1 egg yolk beaten with a pinch of salt, to glaze

a large baking tray, greased

Makes 1 loaf

*To use active dry yeast, add 1 package to the flour with the salt and sugar, then proceed with the recipe.

Heat the milk, sugar, and vanilla bean in a small pan until just steaming. Cover and set aside until the milk is lukewarm. Remove the bean and scrape the seeds into the milk.

In a small bowl, cream the yeast and milk to a smooth liquid. Mix the flour and salt in a bowl, make a well in the center, pour the liquid, butter, and eggs into the well, then mix. Work in the flour to make a soft but not sticky dough. If too dry, add tepid water 1 tablespoon at a time. If sticky and soft, work in flour 1 tablespoon at a time. Turn out on a floured surface and knead for 10 minutes until silky and elastic.

Return to the washed and greased bowl and turn until the surface is lightly coated with oil. Cover with a damp cloth and let rise in a cool spot until doubled in size—1½ to 2 hours. Punch down the dough, cover, and let rise as before—about 45 minutes. Punch down again and knead in the bowl for 1 minute. Let rest in the bowl, covered with the cloth, for 5 minutes. Cover loosely with a damp cloth and let rise as before until doubled in size—about 45 minutes.

Divide and braid the dough as described in the previous recipe. Brush with 2 thin coats of egg-yolk glaze and bake in a preheated oven at 425°F for 10 minutes.

Glaze again and reduce the heat to 375°F and bake for 30 minutes or until the loaf is golden brown and sounds hollow when tapped underneath. Cool on a wire rack.

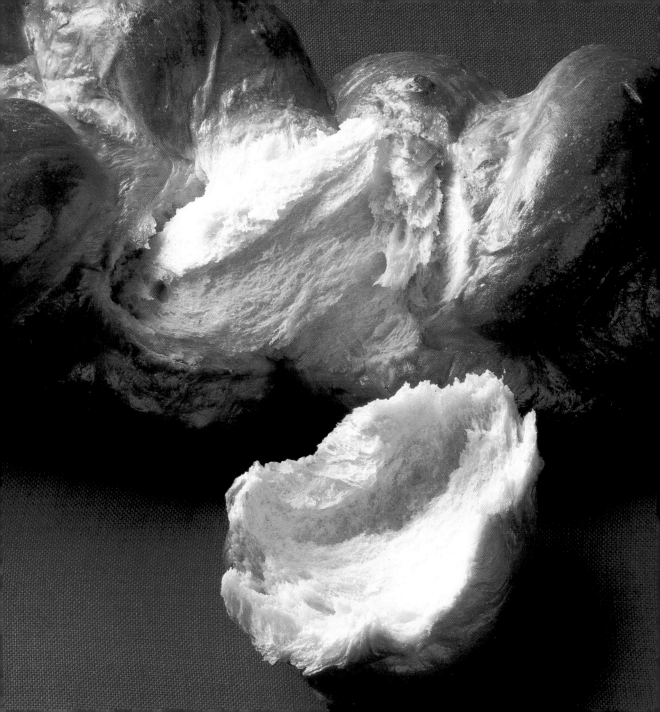

A loaf with the distinctive taste of rye without the heavy texture—stone-ground rye flour will produce the best flavor.

rye and caraway loaf

Mix the two flours, caraway seeds, and salt in a large bowl and make a well in the center.

In a small bowl, cream the yeast to a smooth liquid with a little of the water. Pour into the well with the rest of the water, then mix in the flour to make a soft but not sticky dough. If too sticky, add white flour, 1 tablespoon at a time. If there are dry crumbs in the bottom of the bowl and the dough is stiff and hard to work, add extra water, 1 tablespoon at a time. Turn out onto a lightly floured surface and knead thoroughly for 10 minutes. Return to the bowl, cover with a damp cloth, and let rise until doubled in size—about 2 hours. Punch down the dough with your knuckles, then turn out onto a lightly floured surface. Knead lightly into an oval. With the edge of your hand, make a crease down the middle, then roll the dough over to make a sausage. Put the seam underneath so the top is smooth and evenly shaped. Place on the baking tray, cover, and let rise until doubled in size—about 1 hour. Uncover the loaf and slash the top several times with a very sharp knife. Bake in a preheated oven at 400°F for 15 minutes until golden, then reduce to 375°F and bake for a further 20 to 25 minutes until the loaf sounds hollow when tapped underneath. Cool on a wire rack.

2⅔ cups unbleached white bread flour

1¾ cups rye flour

2 tablespoons caraway seeds

3 teaspoons sea salt

¾ cake compressed yeast, crumbled*

1⅞ cups cold water

extra flour, for dusting

one baking tray, greased

Makes 1 large loaf

To use active dry yeast, mix 1 package with the flours, seeds, and salt. Add the water and proceed with the recipe.

29

*A mixed-flour loaf, **speckled** with dried chile flakes. Wonderful with smoked salmon and cream cheese—the combination of hot, cold, and savory is irresistible.*

chile pepper bread

2–3 teaspoons dried chile flakes, or to taste

1⅔ cups strong white bread flour

1½ cups stone-ground whole-wheat bread flour

1½ cups stone-ground rye flour

3 teaspoons sea salt

¾ cake compressed yeast, crumbled*

1⅛ cups water, at room temperature

extra flour, for dusting

one 2¼ lb. loaf pan, greased

Makes 1 large loaf

To use dried easy-blend yeast, mix 1 package with the chile flakes, flours, and salt. Add all the liquid at once and proceed with the recipe.

Mix the chile pepper, flours, and salt in a large bowl. In a small bowl, cream the yeast until smooth with a little water. Make a well in the flour mixture, pour in the yeast paste and the rest of the water. Gradually work the flour into the liquid to make a soft but not sticky dough. If it sticks to your hands, add a little more white flour. If there are dry crumbs in the bowl and the dough is stiff and hard to work, add water, about 1 tablespoon at a time. Turn out onto a lightly floured surface and knead for 10 minutes until very elastic and pliable. Return to the bowl, cover with a damp cloth, and let rise at cool room temperature until doubled in size—about 2 hours. Punch down the risen dough with your knuckles, then turn out onto a lightly floured surface and shape to fit your pan. Put it in the pan and tuck under the ends to make a neat shape (the top of the dough should be halfway up the sides of the pan). Cover and leave at cool to normal room temperature until the dough rises just above the rim of the pan—about 1½ hours. Bake in a preheated oven at 450°F for about 15 minutes. Reduce to 400°F and cook for 25 to 30 minutes until the loaf sounds hollow when removed from the tin and tapped underneath. Cool on a wire rack.

A *speckled*, airy bread—great with soups and sandwiches.
poppyseed loaf

1¼ oz. poppy seeds

4⅓ cups unbleached white bread flour

2 teaspoons sea salt

½ stick sweet butter, chilled and diced

1½ tablespoons sugar

¾ cake compressed yeast, crumbled*

1⅓ cups skim milk, at room temperature

1 egg, beaten

extra flour, for dusting

extra milk, for brushing

one 2 lb. loaf pan, greased

Makes 1 large loaf

To use active dry yeast, add 1 package to the flour with the salt and poppy seeds, then proceed with the recipe.

Mix the seeds, flour, and salt in a large bowl. Add the butter and rub in with your fingertips until the mixture resembles fine crumbs. Stir in the sugar and make a well in the center. In a small bowl, cream the yeast to a smooth liquid with a little of the milk. Pour into the well with the egg and remaining milk.

Work the flour into the liquid to make a soft but not sticky dough. Turn out onto a lightly floured surface and knead thoroughly for 10 minutes. Return to the bowl, cover with a damp cloth, and let rise at cool to normal room temperature until doubled in size—about 1½ to 2 hours.

Punch down the risen dough, then turn out onto a lightly floured surface. Knead it smooth for 1 minute, then pat into a rectangle the length of the pan and about ½ inch thick. Roll up the dough like a jelly roll from one short end. Pinch the seam with your fingers to seal, then put the dough into the pan, seam side down, tucking the ends underneath. The pan should be half filled. Cover with a damp cloth and let rise at room temperature until doubled in size—about 1 hour.

Uncover and brush with milk. Bake in a preheated oven at 450°F for 15 minutes, reduce to 400°F, and bake for 20 to 30 minutes, until the turned-out loaf sounds hollow when tapped underneath. Cool on a wire rack.

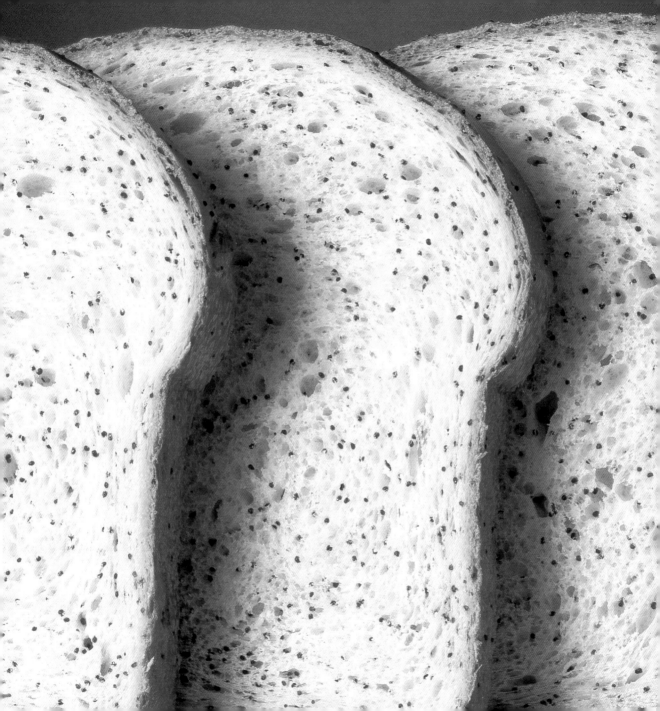

multi-seed bread

Put the flours, seeds (except the garnish), and salt in a large bowl and mix thoroughly. Make a well in the center. In a small bowl, cream the yeast to a smooth liquid with a little of the water. Pour into the well, then add the oil and all but ¼ cup of the water. Gradually work the flour mixture into the liquid to make a soft but not sticky dough, adding more water as necessary. Turn out onto a lightly floured work surface and knead thoroughly for about 10 minutes. Return the dough to the bowl, cover with a damp cloth, and let rise at cool to normal room temperature until doubled in size—about 1½ to 2 hours.

Punch down the dough with your knuckles, turn out of the bowl onto a lightly floured surface, knead for 1 minute, then divide in half. Shape each half to fit a loaf pan, then put into the pans, tucking the ends under—the dough should half-fill each pan. Cover and let rise until doubled in size—about 1 hour. Using a sharp knife, slash the tops several times. Brush both with milk, then sprinkle with the extra seeds. Bake in a preheated oven at 400°F for about 35 minutes until the loaves are golden and sound hollow when turned out and tapped underneath. Cool on a wire rack.

Crammed full of seeds and with plenty of texture and flavor, this dense loaf makes great toast.

3 cups unbleached white bread flour

1⅓ cups spelt flour

¾ oz. poppy seeds

1 oz. linseeds

1 oz. sesame seeds

1 oz. sunflower seeds

1 oz. pumpkin seeds

3 teaspoons sea salt

¾ cake compressed yeast, crumbled*

1¾–2 cups water, at room temperature

1 tablespoon olive oil

extra flour, for dusting

milk, for brushing

extra linseeds and sesame seeds, to finish

two 1 lb. loaf pans, greased

Makes 2 medium loaves

To use active dry yeast, mix 1 package with the flours, add the water, and proceed with the recipe.

molasses and mixed grain
pumpernickel

1½ cups stone-ground rye flour

1 cup coarse stone-ground
whole-wheat bread flour

⅔ cup spelt flour

⅓ cup barley flour

⅓ cup fine oat flour

⅓ cup buckwheat flour

⅔ cup white bread flour

2 teaspoons sea salt

1½ tablespoons dark brown sugar

1 cake compressed yeast,
crumbled*

1½ cups water

2 oz. molasses

1 tablespoon vegetable oil

one 2 lb. loaf pan, greased

Makes 1 large loaf

*To use active dry yeast, mix
1½ packages with the white flour.
Put the other flours, salt, and
sugar in a bowl, make a well, pour
in the water and add yeast mixture.*

Mix the flours, oatmeal, salt, and sugar in a large mixing bowl, and make a well in the center.

In a small bowl, cream the yeast to a smooth liquid together with a little of the water. Stir in the rest of the water, then tip it into the well.

Mix some of the flour into the liquid to make a thick, smooth batter in the well. Sprinkle a little flour over the batter to prevent a skin forming, then cover and leave the bowl for 30 minutes until the batter looks bubbly.

Stir the molasses and oil into the batter, then gradually work in the rest of the flour to make a soft, slightly sticky dough. It will seem heavier and more difficult to work than other bread doughs, but if it is dry or too hard to work, you may need to add a little extra water. If it seems wet or too sticky, add a little extra white flour, 1 tablespoon at a time.

Turn out onto a floured surface and knead thoroughly for about 5 minutes. Cover the dough with an upturned bowl, let rest for about 5 minutes, then knead for a further 5 minutes. Return the dough to the bowl, cover with a damp cloth, and let rise at normal room temperature until doubled in size— about 3 hours.

Punch down the risen dough, then turn out onto a lightly floured work surface and knead for 1 minute. Shape into a loaf to fit the pan, then put in the dough, pushing it into the corners—the top of the dough should be halfway up the pan.

Cover with a damp cloth and let rise at normal room temperature until the dough reaches the top of the pan—about 1½ to 2 hours.

Bake in a preheated oven at 400°F for about 40 minutes or until the loaf is dark brown and sounds hollow when removed from the pan and tapped underneath.

Cool completely on a wire rack, then keep wrapped in greaseproof paper for at least 1 to 2 days before slicing thinly. This loaf will mature when kept and will taste best about 4 days after baking.

Variation

Raisin Pumpernickel

Place ½ cup of raisins or golden raisins in a bowl, pour over orange juice to cover, and let soak for about 1 hour. Drain, then add the fruit to the dough just before shaping into a loaf. Proceed as in the main recipe.

*Molasses produces the traditional dark color in this dense, **rich** bread made with a mixture of flours, predominantly **rye**.*

spelt sourdough

½ cake compressed yeast, crumbled*

2¾ cups water at room temperature

3⅓ cups spelt flour

3 teaspoons sea salt

about 2⅓ cups strong white bread flour

extra flour, for dusting

one large baking tray, floured

Makes 1 large loaf

*I have had variable results with active dry yeast and prefer compressed yeast for this recipe.

Cream the yeast in a bowl with half the water until smooth. Stir in 1¾ cups spelt flour to make a thick batter, cover with a damp cloth, and set aside for 24 hours until it looks bubbly and slightly gray. Next day, stir in the remaining water to make a smooth batter. Transfer to a larger bowl, beat in the salt and remaining spelt flour with your hand, then gradually work in enough white flour to make a soft but not sticky dough (the amount depends on the quality of the spelt flour). Turn out onto a floured surface and knead for 10 minutes. If it sticks to your fingers, work in extra white flour. Return to the bowl, cover with a damp cloth, and let rise at cool to normal room temperature until doubled in size—about 3 hours.

Punch down the dough, turn out onto a floured surface, and knead for 1 minute. It should be firm enough to hold its shape during baking: if too soft, work in extra flour.

Shape into a round loaf and place on the baking tray. Cover loosely and let rise as before until almost doubled in size— about 1½ to 2 hours. Slash the top several times with a sharp knife, sprinkle with white flour, then bake in a preheated oven at 425°F for 20 minutes. Reduce to 400°F and bake for about 15 minutes or until the loaf sounds hollow when tapped underneath. Cool on a wire rack.

Spelt flour has a *nutty* flavor and has recently become popular with *organic* farmers.

coarse whole-wheat
beer bread

2⅔ cups stone-ground
whole-wheat bread flour

⅔ cup coarsely ground
whole-wheat bread flour or
wheaten bread flour

2 teaspoons sea salt

¾ cake compressed yeast,
crumbled*

1 tablespoon lukewarm water

about 1½ cups beer,
at room temperature

extra flour, for dusting

one baking tray, greased

Makes 1 medium loaf

**To use active dry yeast, add
1 package to the flour, then
proceed with the recipe.
Omit the water and add 1 extra
tablespoon of beer.*

Mix the flours and salt in a large bowl. Make a well in the center. In a small bowl, cream the yeast and water to a smooth paste. Add it and the beer to the well in the flour. Mix to a soft but not sticky dough, working it together for several minutes before adding anything else.

The amount of liquid you need will depend on the flour, but the dough will feel very different from a white bread dough. If it seems very wet, add extra flour, 1 tablespoon at a time. If stiff and dry, with dry crumbs in the bottom of the bowl, work in extra beer or water, 1 tablespoon at a time.

Knead for 5 to 7 minutes on a floured surface until the dough is smooth and pliable. Return to the bowl, cover with a damp cloth, and let rise at normal room temperature until doubled in size—about 2 hours.

Punch down the risen dough and shape into a ball. Place on the baking tray, cover loosely with a damp cloth, and let rise again as before until doubled in size—about 1 hour.

Uncover the loaf, slash the top with a sharp knife, sprinkle with coarse whole-wheat flour, and bake in a preheated oven at 425°F for 30 to 35 minutes until the loaf is golden brown and sounds hollow when tapped underneath. Cool on a wire rack.

German-style smoked beer, brown ale, or stout give strongest flavor: pale ale a more subtle taste.

honeynut loaf

2⅛ cups stone-ground
whole-wheat bread flour

2⅓ cups unbleached
white bread flour

2½ teaspoons sea salt

1 cake compressed yeast,
crumbled*

1½ cups water, at room
temperature

3 tablespoons honey

extra flour, for dusting

10½ oz. nuts (any combination of
walnuts, hazelnuts, almonds,
cashews, or macadamias), lightly
toasted and coarsely chopped

2 baking sheets, greased

Makes 2 medium loaves

*To use active dry yeast, mix
1 package with the flour and salt,
add the water and honey, then
proceed with the recipe.*

Mix the flours and salt together in a large mixing bowl and make a well in the center.

Crumble the yeast into a small bowl, then cream with a little of the water until it forms a smooth liquid. Tip the mixture into the well in the flour.

Dissolve the honey in the rest of the water and add it to the well. Gradually work the flour into the liquid to make a soft but not sticky dough.

If the dough sticks to your fingers, work in extra flour, about 1 tablespoon at a time. If there are dry crumbs in the bottom of the bowl—or the dough seems stiff and hard to work—add extra water, 1 tablespoon at a time.

Turn out onto a lightly floured surface and knead thoroughly for 10 minutes until smooth and elastic.

Flatten the dough with your hand, sprinkle about a third of the nuts over the dough, then fold it over and over to distribute them evenly through the mixture.

Repeat this process twice, then shape the dough into a ball, and return it to the bowl.

Cover with a damp cloth and let rise at cool to normal room temperature until doubled in size—about 2 hours.

Punch down the risen dough with your knuckles, then turn out onto a floured surface and knead for 1 minute to ensure the nuts are evenly distributed.

Divide the dough in half. Shape each portion into a neat ball, pushing back any nuts that protrude or escape.

Make this well-flavored bread with any combination of lightly toasted nuts, together with a strong-flavored honey, such as clover. Best served with butter, cream cheese, or cheese.

Place the balls of dough on a baking tray, cover as before, and let rise at cool to normal room temperature until doubled in size—about 1½ hours.

Uncover the risen loaves and slash the tops diagonally several times with a very sharp knife.

Bake in a preheated oven at 425°F for about 15 minutes, then reduce the temperature to 375°F and bake for a further 20 to 25 minutes.

The loaves should sound hollow when removed from the baking tray and tapped underneath. Cool on a wire rack.

Variation

New England Maple Nut Loaf

A wonderful combination of traditional American ingredients; dried cranberries, maple syrup, and pecans.

Omit the roasted nuts from the main recipe and add 3 oz. dried cranberries and 5½ oz. pecans broken into pieces. Substitute 3 tablespoons maple syrup instead of the honey, and proceed as in the main recipe.

Use a good **sugarless** *granola with ingredients such as raisins, dates, wheat flakes, oat flakes, apples, apricots, hazelnuts, almonds, and raisins.*

granola round

Put the flours, muesli, and salt into a large bowl and mix well. Make a well in the center.

In a small bowl, cream the yeast to a smooth liquid with 3 tablespoons of the milk mixture. Stir in the rest of the liquid, the honey, and oil, then pour into the well. Gradually mix the dry ingredients into the liquid to make a fairly firm dough. If it seems dry or stiff, or there are dry crumbs in the bottom of the bowl, work in extra milk or water, 1 tablespoon at a time. If the dough sticks to your fingers, knead in extra white flour, 1 tablespoon at a time. The amount of liquid needed will depend on the muesli mix.

Turn out onto a lightly floured surface and knead for about 5 minutes. Place in the bowl, cover with a damp cloth, and leave at room temperature until doubled in size—1 to 1½ hours. Turn out onto a lightly floured surface and knead for 1 minute. Shape into a round loaf 8 inches across. Put on the prepared baking tray and score into 8 segments with a very sharp knife. Cover and let rise as before—about 1 hour.

Uncover and sprinkle with whole-wheat flour. Cook in a preheated oven at 425°F for 30 minutes, or until it sounds hollow when tapped underneath. Cool on a wire rack.

3⅓ cups strong white bread flour

⅔ cup stone-ground whole-wheat flour

1⅔ cups unsweetened granola or muesli

2 teaspoons salt

¾ cake compressed yeast, crumbled*

about 1¾ cups equal mixture of milk and water, at room temperature

1 tablespoon honey

2 tablespoons vegetable oil

extra flour, for dusting

one baking tray, greased

Makes 1 large round loaf

*To use active dry yeast, mix 1 package with the flours, granola, and salt. Pour in all the liquids, then proceed with the recipe.

blue cheese and
walnut twist

2 cups unbleached
white bread flour

1 teaspoon sea salt

¼ stick butter, chilled and diced

½ cake compressed yeast,
crumbled*

½ cup equal mixture of milk and
water, at room temperature

1 egg, beaten

extra flour, for dusting

Cream Cheese and Walnut Filling:

¾ cup cream cheese

1 tablespoon milk

½ cup finely ground walnuts

freshly ground black pepper

1 cup blue cheese

1 cup walnut pieces

a baking tray, greased

Makes 1 loaf

*To use active dry yeast, mix
2 teaspoons with the flour and salt,
then proceed with the recipe.*

Mix the flour and salt in a large bowl. Rub in the butter with your fingertips until the mixture looks like fine crumbs. Make a well in the center.

In a small bowl, cream the yeast with the milk and water until smooth. Mix in the egg, then pour into the well. Gradually work in the flour to make a soft but not sticky dough.

Turn out onto a floured surface and knead for 10 minutes until smooth, silky, and elastic. Return to the bowl, cover with a damp cloth, and let rise at normal room temperature until doubled in size—about 1 hour.

To make the filling, beat the cream cheese and milk until soft, then beat in the walnuts and pepper. Crumble the blue cheese into small chunks and mix with the walnut pieces. Punch down the risen dough, then roll out on a lightly floured surface into a rectangle, 13 x 12 inches. Spread with the cheese mixture, then sprinkle blue cheese and walnuts over the top.

Roll up the dough fairly tightly from one long side, like a jelly roll, then roll this into a longer, thinner cylinder about 2 feet long. Cut in half lengthwise with a sharp knife. Twist the halves together, cut sides up, and shape into a neat ring on the baking tray.

Cover loosely with a damp cloth and let rise at room temperature until doubled in size—45 minutes to 1 hour.

Bake in a preheated oven at 400°F for 25 minutes, or until firm and golden. Cool on a wire rack.

A flavorful loaf, not too sweet— good with cold meats and pickles.
sour cherry loaf

2⅓ cups unbleached
white bread flour

1 cup rye flour,
stone-ground if possible

½ cup dried sour cherries

2 teaspoons sea salt

¾ cake compressed yeast,
crumbled*

about 1¼ cups water
from the cold tap

extra flour, for dusting

one baking tray, greased

Makes 1 medium loaf

*To use active dry yeast, add
1 package to the flour, then
proceed with the recipe.*

Mix the flours, dried sour cherries, and salt in a large bowl and make a well in the center. In a small bowl, cream the yeast with half the water until smooth. Pour into the well, add the remaining water, then gradually mix in the flour to make a soft but not sticky dough. If it seems sticky and difficult to work, mix in white flour 1 tablespoon at a time. If stiff and dry, with crumbs in the bottom of the bowl, work in water, 1 tablespoon at a time (the amount depends on the quality of the flour). Turn out onto a lightly floured surface and knead for about 10 minutes until satiny and elastic. Return to the bowl, cover with a damp cloth, and let rise at cool to normal room temperature until doubled in size—about 2 hours.

Punch down the dough and turn out onto a lightly floured surface. Gently knead into an oval. With the edge of your hand, make a crease down the middle, then roll the dough over to make a sausage shape about 10 inches long. Place, seam side down, on the baking tray. Cover and let rise at normal room temperature until doubled in size—about 1 hour. Uncover the loaf and slash several times across the top with a very sharp knife.

Bake in a preheated oven at 425°F for 15 minutes until golden. Reduce to 375°F and bake 10 to 15 minutes until the loaf sounds hollow when tapped underneath. Cool on a wire rack.

VEGETABLES **AND CHEESE**

Slow-cooked onion and rye flour give flavor without pungency.

onion rolls

1 large onion, finely chopped

½ teaspoon sugar

¼ stick sweet butter

2⅔ cups strong white bread flour

⅔ cup rye flour,
preferably stone-ground

2½ teaspoons sea salt

¾ cake compressed yeast,
crumbled*

1¼ cups water,
at room temperature

extra flour, for dusting

1 egg, beaten with a pinch
of salt, to glaze

2 greased baking trays

Makes 14

*To use active dry yeast, mix
½ package with the flours and salt,
add the water and onion mixture,
then proceed with the recipe.*

Put the onion, sugar, and butter in a heavy pan and cook slowly, stirring, until soft and slightly caramelized. Cool.

Mix the flours and salt in a bowl and make a well in the center. In a small bowl, cream the yeast with a little water until smooth. Add to the well with the onion and remaining water. Work in the flour to make a soft but not sticky dough. If it sticks to your fingers or the bowl, work in white flour, 1 tablespoon at a time. If it seems stiff, with dry crumbs in the bowl, slowly work in water, 1 tablespoon at a time.

Turn out onto a floured surface and knead for 10 minutes until very smooth and elastic. Return to the bowl, cover with a damp cloth, and let rise at cool to normal room temperature until doubled in size—about 1 to 1½ hours.

Punch down the dough, turn out onto a floured surface, and knead for 1 minute. Weigh and divide into 14 equal pieces. Shape into balls and place well apart on the baking trays. To make the onion shapes, pinch the centers, drawing them up to make a stalk. Cover with a damp cloth—to avoid flattening the stalks, use upturned bowls to support the cloth. Let rise for 30 minutes, until doubled in size.

Brush with egg glaze, then bake in a preheated oven at 425°F for about 15 to 20 minutes until shiny golden brown. Cool on a wire rack.

garlic knots

Put the flour and salt in a large bowl and make a well in the center. In a small bowl, cream the yeast with a little water until smooth. Stir in the oil, tip into the well, then work in the flour to make a soft but not sticky dough. If too sticky, work in extra flour, 1 tablespoon at a time. If there are dry crumbs in the bowl, work in extra water a little at a time. Turn out onto a floured surface and knead for 10 minutes until smooth, silky, and elastic. Return to the bowl, cover with a damp cloth, and let rise at cool to normal room temperature until doubled in size—about 1½ to 2 hours.

Cook the garlic in a preheated oven at 375°F for 10 minutes until the skin is split and golden and the flesh soft and ripe smelling. Cool and peel, add salt, then mash the garlic into a coarse paste with the back of a knife.

Punch down the risen dough, then weigh. Turn out onto a floured surface and divide into 12 equal pieces. Shape into sausages about 8 inches long and flatten slightly. Spread the garlic paste on the top, then tie into knots. Place well apart on the baking trays, cover loosely with a damp cloth, and let rise until doubled in size—about 45 minutes.

Brush with egg glaze, then bake in a preheated oven at 425°F for 10 to 15 minutes until the knots are golden brown and sound hollow when tapped underneath. Cool on a wire rack.

Roasted garlic produces a delicious *aroma* with no harsh taste.

3⅓ cups strong white bread flour

1½ teaspoons sea salt

½ cake compressed yeast, crumbled*

1¼ cups water from the cold tap

1 tablespoon virgin olive oil

12 unpeeled garlic cloves

a pinch of salt

extra flour, for dusting

1 egg, beaten with a pinch of salt, to glaze

two baking trays, greased

Makes 12

*To use active dry yeast, mix ⅔ package with the flour and salt. Proceed with the recipe.

Pumpkin makes a fine, soft, *golden* *bread that toasts well.*

pumpkin bread

Peel the pumpkin and remove the seeds. Dice the flesh into ½-inch cubes—you will need 14 oz.

Without adding water, cook the cubes in a steamer or microwave until they soften. Put them into a food processor with the oil and purée until smooth. Let cool until just lukewarm, then mix in the salt and sugar.

In a small bowl, cream the yeast to a smooth paste with 1 tablespoon of lukewarm water. Mix the paste into the purée.

Put the flour into a large mixing bowl and make a well in the center. Spoon the purée into the well, then mix in the flour to make a soft but not sticky dough. Turn out onto a floured work surface and knead thoroughly for 5 minutes (or 3 minutes at low speed in a mixer with a dough hook).

Shape the dough into a round loaf about 7 inches across and put it on the baking tray. Cover and let rise at normal room temperature until doubled in size—about 1½ hours.

Press your thumb into the middle of the risen loaf to make a small hollow, then carefully brush the loaf with the egg glaze. Score the loaf into segments with a sharp knife, then bake in a preheated oven at 400°F for about 30 minutes until it is golden brown and sounds hollow when tapped underneath.

Cool on a wire rack.

1 lb. 10 oz. pumpkin, Japanese kabocha, or other winter squash

1 tablespoon virgin olive oil

2½ teaspoons sea salt

2 teaspoons sugar

¾ cake compressed yeast, crumbled*

2⅓ cups strong white bread flour

extra flour, for dusting

1 egg, beaten with a pinch of salt, to glaze

a baking tray, greased

Makes 1 medium loaf

To use active dry yeast, mix 1 package with the flour, then work in the pumpkin purée. If the dough seems dry or there are dry crumbs in the bottom of the bowl, work in a little cold water.

easy cheesy brioche

¾ cake compressed yeast*

½ cup lukewarm skim milk

2 eggs

1 teaspoon sea salt

¼ teaspoon cayenne pepper

2 cups strong white bread flour

½ stick sweet butter, softened

1 cup Gruyère cheese, grated,
plus 1 oz. extra, to finish

extra flour, for dusting

1 egg, beaten with a large pinch
of salt, to glaze

one 1 lb. loaf pan, greased

Makes 1 medium loaf

*To use active dry yeast, mix
1 package with the flour and work
into the liquids in the bowl.
Proceed with the recipe.*

Crumble the yeast into the bowl of a free-standing mixer. Pour in the milk and mix with the beater attachment. Beat in the eggs, then the salt and cayenne pepper.

Using the dough hook at low speed, gradually work in the flour to make a soft but not sticky dough. Knead in the machine at low speed for another 5 minutes until smooth and elastic.

Add the softened butter and knead for another 3 to 4 minutes until completely incorporated. Cover and let rise at normal room temperature until doubled in size—about 1½ hours.

Knead the grated cheese into the dough for about 1 minute at slow speed, then turn out onto a floured surface and shape into a loaf to fit the pan.

Put in the pan, then cover with a damp cloth and leave at normal room temperature until doubled in size—about 1 hour (the dough should just reach the rim of the pan).

Gently brush the risen loaf with egg glaze, taking care not to glue it to the sides of the pan.

Sprinkle with the extra cheese and bake in a preheated oven at 400°F for about 35 minutes until it turns golden brown and sounds hollow when turned out and tapped underneath. Cool on a wire rack.

A rich, light, *tangy* loaf—and *easily* made in a mixer, unlike a classic brioche. Serve it with cheese, salad, or soup.

cheese rolls
with cheddar and onion

4⅓ cups unbleached
white bread flour

2 teaspoons sea salt

1 teaspoon powdered mustard

1½ cups cheddar cheese, grated

1½ oz. scallions, finely chopped

¾ cake compressed yeast,
crumbled*

⅔ cup skim milk,
at room temperature

⅔ cup water, at room temperature

extra flour, for dusting

oil, for greasing bowl

milk, for glazing

½ cup mature cheddar cheese,
for sprinkling

2 baking trays, lightly greased

Makes 12

*To use active dry yeast, add
1 package to the flour, then
proceed with the recipe.

Mix the flour, salt, mustard, cheese, and onions in a large bowl. Make a well in the center.

In a small bowl, cream the yeast to a smooth liquid with the milk, then stir in the water. Pour into the well in the flour. Gradually work the flour into the liquid to make a soft but not sticky dough.

Turn out onto a floured surface and knead for 10 minutes until it feels smooth and elastic. It can also be kneaded for 5 minutes at low speed in a mixer fitted with a dough hook.

Put the dough into a lightly greased bowl, turning it so the entire surface is lightly coated with oil. Cover with a damp cloth and let rise until doubled in size—1½ to 2 hours.

Punch down the dough, then turn out onto a floured surface and knead for a few seconds. Divide into 12 and pat into ovals about 4½ x 3 x 1 inch. Arrange well apart on the baking trays. Brush with milk, then sprinkle with cheese. Let rise until doubled in size—about 30 minutes.

Press your thumb into the middle of each bap, then bake in a preheated oven at 425°F for 15 minutes until golden. Cool on a wire rack.

For the best flavor, use *sharp cheese: much so-called cheddar is too bland for this recipe.*

INDEX

bacon and walnut fougasses 12
basil, cherry tomato focaccia with, 16
beer bread, coarse whole-wheat 42
blue cheese and walnut twist 50
brioche, easy cheese 60

caraway loaf, rye and 29
cheddar, cheese rolls with onion 62
cheese:
   blue, and walnut twist 50
   rolls with cheddar and onion 62
   easy cheesy brioche 60
cherry, sour, loaf 52
chile pepper bread 30
challah, vanilla 26
ciabatta, Italian, with olives and thyme 19
coarse whole-wheat beer bread 42

easy cheese brioche 60

flours:
   malted brown 7
   oatmeal 38
   rye 7
   spelt 7
   stone-ground 7
   strong white bread 7
   whole-wheat 7
focaccia:
   cherry tomato with basil 16
   with pancetta 16
   with rosemary and sea salt 14
fougasses:
   bacon and walnut 12
   salami 13

garlic knots 57
granola round 49

honeynut loaf 46

Italian ciabatta with olives and thyme 19

kabocha 58
knots, garlic 56

maple, New England nut loaf 47
molasses and mixed grain
      pumpernickel 38
multi-seed bread 35

New England maple nut loaf 46
nuts:
   bacon and walnut fougasses 12
   blue cheese and walnut twist 50
   honeynut loaf 46
   muesli round 48
   New England maple nut loaf 47

olives:
   olive oil bread 20
   Italian ciabatta with olives and
      thyme 19
onion:
   cheese rolls with cheddar and 62
   rolls 56

pancetta, focaccia with 16
poppyseed loaf 32
pumpernickel, molasses and mixed
      grain 38
pumpkin bread 58

raisin pumpernickel 38
rolls:
   cheese, with cheddar and onion 62
   onion 56
rosemary and sea salt focaccia 14
rye and caraway loaf 29

saffron braided loaf 24
salami fougasses 13
sea salt, focaccia with 14
sour cherry loaf 52
sourdough bread, spelt 40
spelt sourdough bread 40

thyme, Italian ciabatta with olives and 18
tomato, cherry, focaccia with basil 16

vanilla challah 26

walnut:
   blue cheese and, twist 50
   and bacon fougasses 12

yeast 7

Conversion Chart

Weights and measures have been rounded up or down slightly to make measuring easier.

volume equivalents:

american	metric	imperial
1 teaspoon	5 ml	
1 tablespoon	15 ml	
¼ cup	60 ml	2 fl.oz.
⅓ cup	75 ml	2½ fl.oz.
½ cup	125 ml	4 fl.oz.
⅔ cup	150 ml	5 fl.oz. (¼ pint)
¾ cup	175 ml	6 fl.oz.
1 cup	250 ml	8 fl.oz.

weight equivalents: **measurements:**

imperial	metric	inches	cm
1 oz.	25 g	¼ inch	5 mm
2 oz.	50 g	½ inch	1 cm
3 oz.	75 g	¾ inch	1.5 cm
4 oz.	125 g	1 inch	2.5 cm
5 oz.	150 g	2 inches	5 cm
6 oz.	175 g	3 inches	7 cm
7 oz.	200 g	4 inches	10 cm
8 oz.	250 g	5 inches	12 cm
9 oz.	275 g	6 inches	15 cm
10 oz.	300 g	7 inches	18 cm
11 oz.	325 g	8 inches	20 cm
12 oz.	375 g	9 inches	23 cm
13 oz.	400 g	10 inches	25 cm
14 oz.	425 g	11 inches	28 cm
15 oz.	475 g	12 inches	30 cm
16 oz. (1 lb.)	500 g		
2 lb.	1 kg		

oven temperatures:

225°F	110°C	Gas ¼
250°F	120°C	Gas ½
275°F	140°C	Gas 1
300°F	150°C	Gas 2
325°F	160°C	Gas 3
350°F	180°C	Gas 4
375°F	190°C	Gas 5
400°F	200°C	Gas 6
425°F	220°C	Gas 7
450°F	230°C	Gas 8
475°F	240°C	Gas 9